UNDER A KANSAS SKY

By
MAUREEN LUBY CUMMINS

Edited by
MICHELE LUBY ELDREDGE

Second Printing

Author
Maureen Luby Cummins
www.scarsusa.com

Editor
Michele Luby Eldredge

Cover & Graphic design by: Dianne C. Dementi

Publisher
Wayne Dementi
Dementi Milestone Publishing, Inc.
Manakin-Sabot, VA 23103
www.dementimilestonepublishing.com

Cataloging-in-publication data for this book is available from The Library of Congress.

ISBN: 978-0-9992891-4-3

Printed in the USA

About the Author

Maureen Luby Cummins was born in Washington D.C., the daughter of a career Naval officer and graduate of the U.S. Naval Academy. She and her sister , Michele, grew up living all over the world. Maureen attended high schools in Norfolk, Virginia; Long Beach, California; Yokohama, Japan and Alexandria, Virginia. She graduated from Longwood University in Virginia with a degree in English and has a master's degree as a reading specialist from Washburn University, Topeka, Kansas.

Maureen has been on the board of directors for four humane societies, an abuse investigator for multiple counties, director of a city humane society, taught Freshman Composition part time at Highland Junior College, and was an English teacher at Topeka West High School for twenty five years.

In addition, she is the state representative on the Pet Animal Advisory Board for licensed shelters and rescues. She has been selected twice as a woman of excellence in Shawnee County for her humane society work, and she and her husband were selected as Capitol Federal Citizens. SCARS was featured in *Dog Fancy* magazine, Cesar's Way, Topeka magazine, and on the front page of the *Topeka Capital Journal* newspaper.

Maureen lives in Auburn, Kansas, is married to Terry Cummins, a CPA, and has a married daughter, Meredith, a son-in-law, Bryan, and a ten year old grandson, Evan.

She is the Operations Manager of SCARS, a no kill sanctuary for homeless dogs.

About the Editor

Michele Luby Eldredge was born in Boston, Massachusetts, and is the author's older sister.

She attended Randolph Macon Women's College in Lynchburg, Virginia, UCLA and George Mason University, Fairfax, Virginia, where she received a BA and MA in English Literature.

Michele has one married son who has been the curator for the Sequoia and King's Canyon National Parks in California since 1998.

TABLE OF CONTENTS

Prologue

Our father graduated from the U. S. Naval Academy in 1938 and spent most of the next 30 years at sea. Like most Navy families we never put down any roots— we were tumbleweeds.

My only time spent with animals were summers when my sister and I visited my mother's family in Virginia. This was heaven for two citified Navy Juniors. An ever changing complement of dogs would run down the driveway to greet us when we arrived, and there was always a basket of kittens in the laundry room. My aunt and uncle also had a magnificent Tennessee Walking Horse named Allen who lived in the stable behind the house and was spoiled by all the cousins. Allen was high spirited with experienced riders, but seemed to know when he had small cargo on board. Our favorite picture is of our cousin Robin (age four) in full cowboy regalia perched atop Allen and looking perfectly in control. But when my sister saddled up, they were off to some galloping worthy of King of the Wind. I loved riding too, but Michele was obsessed. She read every horse book in the library, and when we lived in London, she drove everyone crazy waiting for the next edition of the *Black Stallion* to be sent from the states. I loved the book *Stuart Little,* so a mouse was my only close association with an "animal!"

When I was a sophomore in high school, we moved from Long Beach, California, in the middle of the year, to the base in Yokosuka, Japan. Michele remained back at UCLA to finish up the semester before coming out to join the family. There were some burglaries on the base and mother got it into her head to purchase a French Poodle when my father was at sea. She named him Sukoshi (pronounced Skoshi) which meant "little" in Japanese. He was a difficult dog-- he bit most of us if something bugged him and that was just about everything. Sometimes walking into the room was reason enough for a kamikaze attack. Years later I asked mother why they did not get rid of him since I have daily phone calls wanting to surrender dogs for crimes less severe than Sukoshi's. She looked shocked and said "but he was our responsibility." This attitude of accountability seems scarce in our world today. Sukoshi lived to be seventeen and his disposition never improved, but my parents grieved deeply when he was gone.

Maureen and Sukoshi in Japan

I still knew little to nothing about animals until several moments of enlightenment when I became an adult.

The first moment was sitting in the kitchen of our home in McLean, Virginia, when Michele was bemoaning the fate of the harp seals in Alaska. In my naivete, I asked her what she was talking about and learned more than I wanted to know. I have never forgotten.

The next time animals invaded my mental world was when my first husband, daughter and I moved to Puerto Rico and lived in a beautiful house overlooking the ocean.

After a few months, I began noticing the dogs roaming the island. Most were starving and mange ridden (sasna) inhabiting the beaches and parking lots. I wanted to help them. My definition of helping was to go to the neighborhood mercado, buy packages of hot dogs and pass them out to the stray dogs lying around.

I often came home crying. Their faces and broken bodies haunted me day and night. When I called my sister back in the states, she advised me to focus on saving who I could in my own little corner of the world. I could not save them all. It was good advice, but hard to follow.

The owners of the villa up the hill had a huge German shepherd who had given birth to countless litters of puppies. The last survivor of her most recent litter was a puppy named Chispita, (little spark, or Sparky as we would say) and she was ravaged with mange and severely malnourished. I had no idea what to do when the mother and puppy would come down the driveway to our house, hungry.

I was learning to speak Spanish with my friend and cleaning lady with whom I could discuss dirty clothes and dogs. Taking her advice my daughter and I loaded the puppy into the car and headed to a veterinary clinic in the mountains. We sat on folding chairs, were given a piece of paper with a number written on it, and waited for the veterinarian. When it was our turn, he gave me some strong white cream to put on her with rubber gloves and apply every three days to cure the painful mange.

Chispa slowly began to improve and gain weight, and I realized I was becoming attached to her. After asking the owners if we could buy her, they gladly gave the puppy to us for free.

Shortly after that we heard gun shots outside of our house. Alarmed, we found out the owner of the villa was shooting at a stray blonde Lab mix puppy seen rummaging in the trash. I was horrified and managed to run outside to catch the dog, and carried him safely into our house where he was fed and bathed. My daughter named him Charlie after a dog in a children's book, and he joined our growing family. Charlie and Chispa became best friends.

To my credit, I accomplished what I thought to be impossible. I convinced the owners to let me get the mother German Shepherd spayed. She stayed on with her owners, but her days of being a puppy machine were finally over.

And when our plane took off from San Juan, we had two hitchhikers aboard. They were the first to be rescued, but not the last. I had merely dipped my toe into the tsunami.

Acknowledgements

Last summer, while I was back in Virginia visiting my beloved mother, we had dinner at Landini's Italian restaurant in Old Towne Alexandria with Navy friends, Tom Church and Melissa McDowell and her husband. Our fathers were classmates at the Naval Academy, and we all grew up together in the far reaches of the world. Tom and I went to three of the same high schools: California, Japan and Virginia. He is a retired Three-Star Admiral from the Naval Academy, and Melissa's husband is a retired Colonel out of West Point. I was in good company.

During dinner, Tom looked at me and said, "You need to write a book, Maureen. You have a goldmine of stories back there in Kansas." I told him I was too busy, as I had told many other people who had made the same suggestion, but a tiny idea flickered in my head and I thought, "Ok, maybe he is right."

When mother passed away this year, my sister and I began sharing dog stories back and forth on email. Michele has a master's degree in English Literature, and I have a master's degree as a Reading Specialist. We could write a book, couldn't we?

So, here it is. This is a collection of stories about a few dogs who have shared their lives with me over the years. These are but a small sampling of those voices who have taught me so much, and have graced my life with joy and sorrow. It is my hope that you will read and enjoy the ones I have chosen, and come to love each featured dog as we do.

And I have so many people to thank along the way.

Thank you, Tom, for lighting the fire in me. I listened to you.

Thank you, Terry, for financially supporting an almost impossibly expensive endeavor. You have never said no to a dog in need. I know I have pushed the envelope in begging for help with some difficult and expensive situations, and you have always come through.

Thank you, Michele, for spending endless hours on your quirky computer, your marvelous writing skills and for breaking all of your rules and adopting Pippa, a stubborn, adorable and determined little French Bull Dog. Her life held scant promise until the day she landed in your capable and loving hands.

Thank you, Lisa Hess, for your endless hours of helping me edit every word and for standing watch over this menagerie for seven + years. Oh yes, and thank you for sharing your four children who have beaten a path up and down our gravel road.

Thank you, Pedro Irigonegaray, for counseling me during some difficult times and for your invaluable advice when it comes to saving dogs: "Maureen, always do what you think to be right." You are my hero.

Thank you, Dr. Jernigan, for always being there for me when I had urgent questions about our dogs. Even though you are far away, I know you are standing by with your incredible diagnostic abilities.

Thank you to our Virginia cousins, Robin and Bo, for directing us to the path of Dementi Press.

Thank you Wayne Dementi for taking a chance on a book written in flyover country.

Thank you to both the Auburn Veterinary Clinic and Companion Animal Clinic for your skill, expertise, and compassion with an endless procession of discarded dogs.

Thank you to our wonderful staff and volunteers for the love and compassion you spend on the broken souls who stagger through our gates. You know who you are.

Thank you to the Topeka community for your invaluable support.

Special thanks go to my colleagues at Topeka West High School who have continued to bring students to our sanctuary, have fundraisers, have weddings and most of all, adopt our dogs.

Thank you, Julie McCarter, your photos are miraculous.

Thank you to Wayne DeLoria and his wife Julie, who have continued to keep up our website and newsletter which is responsible for saving hundreds of lives.

Thank you to Staci Williams and staff for your generous donations of canned dog food and toys.

Thank you, DB, you were the light of my life.

Thank you, Meredith, you are always a voice of reason and my best friend.

Thank you to my wonderful parents, both of whom are together in heaven, for instilling the highest values in me.

But most of all, thank you to all the furry faces who have looked up at me with eyes that said , "Please help me." That I am able to reach out and offer a respite from your pain is my greatest joy.

I chose this as the first story because I met my husband, Terry, through this dog. Terry shares my love for animals, and without him, there would be no sanctuary, no place for these lost souls to find a sheltering sky.

Cupid in Disguise

The stifling heat of a Kansas summer was upon us, and ominous warnings for the elderly and animals were issued on TV and the radio. We moved slowly, breathlessly, hoping for cooling breezes. Trees were immobilized by the relentless heat, grass turned brown and the earth cracked. The sun burned everything, rose too early and stayed too long.

In a back yard, a reddish brown husky with gold eyes was forgotten. With a chain wrapped around his hind leg, no shade or water, he waited for relief. His owner, unconcerned about the 105 degree heat, slept in his air conditioned room, the whir of the motor silencing intermittent cries from the dog in his yard. The hours dragged on and Jake faltered and collapsed.

It was almost too late when the abuse was reported. The own-

1

er, ordered by the police to take his dog to the vet, did so and promptly disappeared. The fight to save Jake began in earnest. He was comatose from heat stroke, and as he began coming around, the vet noticed a dark area on his leg where the chain had cut off the circulation. Gangrene had set in.

The doctor was now faced with a problem. If he amputated the leg, it would be at his expense. Finding a home for a healthy animal was not always easy, much less a three legged one. The leg would have to come off if he was to live, so he made his decision. Jake's luck was beginning to change.

Several years ago when I was with the McPherson Humane Society, I had dealt with a similar situation. A family had surrendered a blonde, shaggy dog who looked like Sandy from the Broadway show "Annie." She had been run over by a car, and her two back legs had atrophied. After four years of living with her owners, she was unceremoniously dumped because of her handicap. Knowing the power of the press, I entered the newspaper office with Sandy in my arms and was informed by an officious secretary that "dogs were not allowed in the building." Pretending not to hear, I headed down the hall, entered the reporter's office, and set Sandy down. A week later she had a home.

Now Jake needed help, and I needed another reporter. I thought of an animal lover who worked at the Topeka Capitol Journal and went in armed with pictures of Jake. He said he would get right on it. "Put on your three dancing shoes, Jake, you're going to be a star!"

A few mornings later, the story broke on the front page. Mist from the night still lingered around the trees, the air was close - it was going to be another hot one. I squinted in the early morning sun and picked up the newspaper which had been thrown haphazardly against the gate. There was no mistaking the headline, "Lucky to be alive Husky awaits a loving home." It was a good story. The picture showed me smiling at Jake, his ears pricked, his eyes bright and hopeful.

I wondered if anyone would respond, or would people assume someone else would call. I didn't have to wonder for long; my phone was ringing when I got home. The first caller was a CPA with a big house, 50 acres securely fenced and five dogs. He had seen Jake's picture in the newspaper and wanted to adopt him. "Did I come with the dog?" I told him no on both counts—five dogs were enough for one man, and I wasn't looking to get adopted. But I did agree to go out with him.

We now had the easiest task in animal rescue, three or four viable homes to choose from. The vet and I finally decided on a family with a fenced yard, two daughters, two dogs, three cats and a lot of love.

Jake, my friend, Linda, and I got in the car for our trip to his new home. I tied a bright blue ribbon around his neck as I always did when dogs were adopted.

As I drove, Jake rested his head on Linda's shoulder as she whispered words of encouragement in his ear. He was ready to try again, and this time he would be in good hands. Linda kissed his trusting face as we drew nearer to our destination. I silently thanked everyone who had played a part in saving this dog.

When we pulled up into the driveway, the girls were hanging over the porch railing, each holding a new toy. I stopped the car, opened the door, and Jake jumped out. He faltered, regained his balance, and ran crookedly toward them with the ribbon around his neck untying and trailing behind him in the dust.

Three years later, I married that CPA, and we embarked on round the clock dog rescue. You might say Jake was really Cupid in disguise.

Them Lollapaloozas

I pulled over to the side of the road, stopped the car and rested my head on the steering wheel. I was lost again. How many years had I been in Kansas? I still didn't get the mile marker thing, and why aren't there any road signs? I read my directions again, left on the Harveyville Road, second road south on Eight Mile Road, (whatever that means), to Bell's Pig Farm. Shirley told me there would be a silver sign, but keep going. Go past Bradford Road and turn north, (whatever happened to good old left and right?) Go two more miles to a house with a blue roof. I had made it as far as the pig farm, but no house with a blue roof. The rain had turned the roads into what Kansans call gumbo. A fitting name for what was now creeping around my tires in the middle of nowhere. The two Lhasa Apsos, whose destiny was in my hands, were snoozing in the sun in the back of the van.

I reached for my cell phone. "Hi Shirley, this is Maureen Cummins, and I think I am lost." I tried to describe my location as best I could in the absence of identifying anything tangible other than a faded wooden fence and some waddling geese. "A pond should be on my right?" I asked. And look for Stratton Boulevard? Well, there is no pond unless it is hiding under all of that brush. I did pass Bell's Pig Farm, and there was a gravel lane through a wheat field. "THAT was Stratton Boulevard?" I had seen a sign on a gravel road that was about a quarter of a mile long ending at two metal sheds. I turned the motor on and backed up while Shirley waited on the phone. I drove back to the gravel driveway, and the sign ambitiously proclaimed, Stratton Boulevard. That was a stretch to say the least. "OK, I think I am here" I said.

She said she would meet me at the intersection (could one call it that) of Stratton Boulevard and the highway. I am not sure I would call this road a highway, remembering my many years driving in Washington D.C.

While waiting, rather praying, to be found in this isolated spot, I thought about how the little Lhasa Apsos in the back seat had ended up in my charge.

A week ago, they had been turned over to me in the parking lot of our favorite Mexican restaurant where Terry and I went every Friday night. This was one luxury we afforded ourselves, and Terry said the fact that the Margaritas scalded all the way down helped erase the stress of the week. Actually, when he polished off two, he decided he loved his job and could definitely make it through another tax season. In this rosy light he wondered why, just yesterday, he had considered selling the practice and moving to Tahiti. So, while Terry ate nachos in the glow of his Margaritas, I kept peering out the window of the restaurant. I can do this, I told myself. It won't be too hard. I can take three more. Let's see, how many does that make? 45? 50?

My friend, Janie, needed help with these dogs, and I wasn't too good at saying no. She had called and begged me to take two Lhasas and a Jack Russell Terrier whose owner had passed away. The good news was they sounded adoptable, at least as opposed to my normal rescues who were usually mixes of questionable origin without shots and never neutered or spayed. It was tax time, and we were overloaded with dogs, I was perpetually exhausted, and Terry was rarely home. "Okay," I said, "We'll take them."

I looked out the window again, and saw Janie standing under a street light with three little dogs. She smiled sheepishly, since a month ago she had saddled me with a killer Corgi who was erroneously named Angel, but that is another story.

On close inspection, the new pups were indeed precious. The Lhasas were wagging their tails furiously, although they were heavily matted, and the Jack Russell was adorable but visibly trembling. I was glad I had said yes.

Looking rather mellow, Terry came out of the restaurant after paying the bill. He helped me load our three new orphans into the car, and we headed home. Launching into our usual drill when we arrived, we found a place for them in an already overcrowded house, got them fed, and tried to get some sleep.

The next day, I made a few phone calls and actually found a home for the terrier, but the Lhasas proved to be more challenging. They had to stay together and cried miserably if separated. Since our website was still in the early stages of development, I decided to advertise in the local paper. In the past, I had actually found some good homes this way as long as I carefully screened the callers. Some of them were downright entertaining, with the most memorable being the lady who asked, "Do you still have them Lollapaloozas?"

This all brings me back to my dubious position waiting for Shirley on Stratton Boulevard aka a muddy gravel road. She finally pulled up in a battered old truck, got out and strode over to my car. Like most farmers' wives, she was casually dressed and still wearing her apron, which gave her a homey appeal. "Honey, don't blame yourself, my husband says I give horrible directions. Well, look at them little darlins. They look just like my babies I used to have." At this point, Cutie and Stinky were jumping up and down, looking very fetching and putting on a good show. (I called him Stinky due to his rather odiferous intestinal problems.)

Shirley snuggled with them for a minute, and then told me to follow her to the house where her husband would be sitting on the porch. "Brad's got cancer, so he is home all day, and I cook for the mental health center near here." I felt immediately concerned that Brad would not be around long, but at least she would have the dogs to keep her company. She later told me he had had cancer for fifteen years, so maybe my concern was unwarranted.

The dirt from her truck swirled around my van as we took a circuitous route, ending up at a humble stone house where an elderly man was sitting lump style in a metal chair. My goodness, that can't be comfortable, I thought to myself. When I got out, a well fed and healthy puppy came running up to me. Shirley told me someone had dumped him at the only gas station in town, so she brought him home. The tightness in my chest was easing up.

She invited me into her house, which was clean and cozy. The walls were covered with pictures of her grandchildren at every month of their development. I could imagine her baking pies for her large family in her gingham apron.

We went over the adoption agreement, I gave her the medical records and headed for home. I thought to my-self while driving along the gravel roads, how wonderful is the bond between animals and humans. Those two little dogs and the good farmers were going to be just fine.

The PTSD Dog

On a normally quiet street on a summer afternoon in Topeka, Kansas, a woman looked out of her window and saw some laughing boys brandishing broomsticks at something in the yard and laughing loudly. She thought this looked like trouble and called the police. Three boys, bravely armed with a roll of duct tape, had a puppy secured to a tree, his eyes and nose taped shut, legs hog tied, rendered helpless while they beat him with long, jagged sticks.

The familiar sound of sirens sent the boys running and the puppy, though injured, was spared. He ended up in the understaffed, underfunded, overpopulated local pound. But it was better than being beaten with sticks, and they gave him food and water.

Shortly after his arrival at the pound, one of the volunteers called me who knew about SCARS and was aware that many of our dogs, deemed unadoptable at local pounds, were transferred to us. Would we please take this poor dog? He was terrified at the shelter and was shutting down. He did deserve a chance, didn't he, especially after what he had been through.

As a licensed shelter director, I had no trouble getting Max released to us, so my husband and I brought

Max home. He was a beautiful Belgian Shepherd mix, with a gold and tan muzzle and a fluffy tan coat. Max was truly one of the prettiest dogs I have ever seen, and he remained with us for 15 years.

We adored him, his precious face and the way he danced around with toys in his mouth. But our dogs, 50 or more, have to get along or chaos will reign. Max seemed determined not to fit in with the group. He was continually starting fights and never winning. Inevitably, humans were bitten while trying to save him. I broke up a fight between him and our St. Bernard right before I was getting ready to leave for the Kansas City airport to pick up my 95 year old mother flying in from Washington DC. After collecting my mother and delivering her to my daughter's house, I headed for the emergency room where I received twenty stitches and was sent on my way. This was a fairly typical episode when one shared life with Max.

In time I found what I thought would be the perfect forever home for Max. A young college girl had fallen in love with him when she visited, and we set up a time for her to adopt him. She owned a nice little house in town with a fenced yard, and would be home off and on during the day. She loved taking walks, and it seemed to be a perfect fit for him. Three days later they were back – Max with his new collar and leash and his new owner with a wad of soggy Kleenex. Max had "shut down." He would not eat, he acted erratically, he shook for no reason, he couldn't adjust to a new environment, he had to come back to SCARS. When we got him out of the van and set him in the driveway in front of the house, he did not move. His eyes were fixed and he did not recognize any of us, not even the other dogs. We brought him into the house and put him back on his favorite bed where he finally fell asleep. Gradually he began to thaw and a week or so later he started to act normal again.

I wish I had known then what I know now. Max had PTSD. In those days not much was known about this condition in people, much less dogs, but today the research is staggering—mostly about the dogs of war but also family pets and rescued dogs in particular. Stacks of research studies; legions of veterinarians, pyschologists, and animal behaviorists checking in; grateful testimonials from readers, tales of success and failure—it's all there and more. This information would have enlightened us—his erratic aggression, "shutting down," failure to thrive in the outside world, virtual unadoptability. We would not have treated Max differently, but it has helped us understand his behavior. Canine PSTD has been traced to a variety of experiences, everything from falling off a chair to being separated from a loved one. Surely the trauma suffered by Max as a puppy puts him in the front of that queue.

Although Max caused chaos among our dog population, he adored kids and they loved him in return. When a girl scout troop came out to play with the dogs and chose a dog to sponsor in a fund raising drive, they chose Max. Dressing him in a black bow tie, the girls hovered around him and made him their poster dog. He had an aura about him that no one could resist and this troop was no exception.

As Max eased into middle age there were fewer fights, he was definitely slowing down and everyone was glad, especially me and the emergency room doctor.   Meanwhile, life went on at our ranch and Max grew older along with us. His limp got worse so I increased his arthritis meds. His back legs became bowed and his muzzle, once glossy black, turned gray. One day I noticed he had not eaten his dinner. He still kept his favorite rope toy in his mouth, but I knew his time with us was drawing to a close. A few days later he was sleeping on his bed, and did not wake up.

Research on canine PTSD stresses the dogs' need for "a safe place." Here at SCARS we promise to keep them safe.   In his case, that was the most and the least we could do.

Writing this story tugged at my heartstrings. I dreamt about Max last night. He was asleep in the corner of my bedroom on the air conditioner vent with his favorite rope toy. In the morning he was gone, of course…… but the toy was still there. I wonder if he will remember to come back and get it.

.

Marvin and Eden
a love story

18

Prince Charming

Every now and then the stars align and a higher power takes over. This certainly was the case with a little Chinese girl with anxiety and a dying Mastiff on the other side of town. Eden had been left at a bus stop in China at five days of age. She was adopted by a loving American family, but she had issues related to her long ago abandonment. Marvin had been unceremoniously dumped in a neighbor's yard, starving and near death. The neighbor could not afford to keep him and called SCARS.

"Mary," I said, as we sat on the wooden porch that was littered with broken toys, "this dog is dying." As I looked down at the emaciated brindle dog lying on the porch, unable to stand, I told her, "If you surrender him to our rescue, we will do everything in our power to save him, but he must go to the vet immediately." I pulled out a wrinkled surrender form that I had stuffed in my pocket. The look in his eyes told me this was a dog worth saving.

Jenny, my faithful volunteer who had come with me, helped me carry him to our car, and we headed for the nearest vet. The clinic staff went into immediate action. He was weighed, a mere 17 pounds for a full grown mastiff mix male. Then came the diagnosis of multiple ailments typical of a dog who has never had a pill or a shot or a decent meal—whipworms, hookworms, round-worms, a bleeding ulcer and complications from starvation. He was put on IV fluids and given multiple medications, and I was told he would be there for at least a week.

The crisis finally passed, and Marvin was allowed to finish his rehab at SCARS, knowing he would receive round the clock care. Never far from where I was working, Marvin watched the world go by. And this world was full of dogs—running, playing, even swimming. He wondered if he would ever be strong enough to join the group. Every now and then a car arrived, and a family left with a dog, everyone smiling and taking pictures of their new family member.

A few months later, I had a call from Eden's mother. Kathryn had been given my name from a friend who knew of SCARS. Kathryn was frantic and exhausted. Eden had been doing fine until the last year or so when she began showing signs of anxiety and depression. Eden would be entering the first grade and needed her rest, as did the family, but everyone was exhausted from the endless hours trying to calm the distressed child in the night.

Eden was afraid of loud noises and generally unable to navigate her world. Her mother wondered if a dog would help. Of course, I knew the kind of dog she had in mind, and it wasn't Marvin. But he had come a long way—healthy, well fed, social, good looking—a real gentle giant. And no one had tried to adopt him. Besides, I had a plan.

Eden's mother met us at the door. "Oh no, we want a small dog—maybe a poodle or a Yorkie—someone Eden can carry around and dress up. You know, a companion. This dog looks rather ferocious." We persuaded her to take Marvin on a trial basis. That night he slept in Eden's bed, and she didn't have any nightmares. The next night, she read him stories. The next day, she took his picture to school and showed her teacher. "This is my new dog. He got left, too." The die was cast. Marvin was staying.

A few weeks later, I stopped by to see how they were doing, and I peeked out the window. I saw Eden doing cartwheels over Marvin's back. He was standing perfectly still so as not to disrupt her performance. Both had been given a new lease on life, but sometimes it takes a village: the family who adopted Eden and were willing to take a chance on Marvin; the neighbor who tried to save him but had the sense to call for help; the vets who spent a week on intensive care bringing him back to life; the owners of SCARS who dipped into their bank account, and the staff and volunteers who kept vigil over his recovery. But it was Eden who crowned him with flowers and transformed him into Prince Charming.

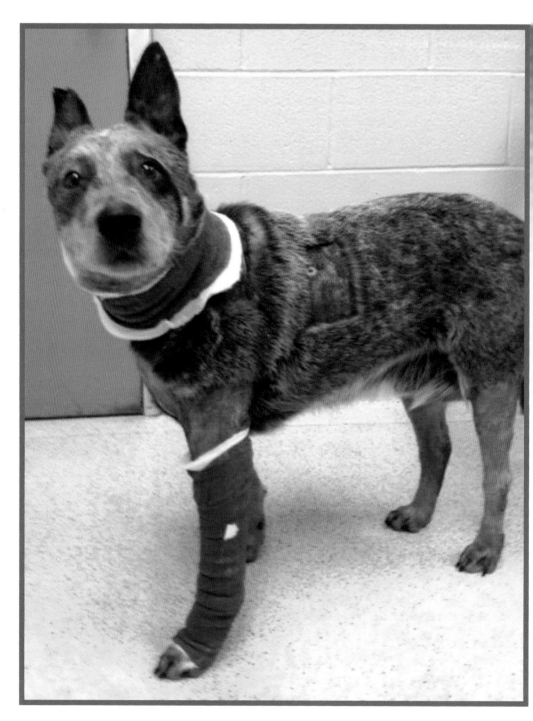

Ghost Dog

One morning when I looked out of the window on an early spring snowfall, my eyes fell on a ghostly shadow drifting across the lower pasture and disappearing into the brush. I looked again, and decided it must have been a mirage.

But then our day manager, Lisa, came in looking worried and said "There's a strange dog in the north pasture." So it was not a mirage after all. This was a recipe for disaster, and we headed outside to search for him. Later, we discovered he had taken refuge in the ravine behind our huge pond. The descent was about 60 feet and at the bottom was heavy brush making an easy place for a dog to hide. And hide he did, for almost a year.

It scared us to have a stray dog loose on our 50 acres. In time, we realized that someone had pushed him through the cattle gate, which was dangerous. When we get new dogs, we integrate each one carefully until they are "one of the pack." Otherwise, our current resident dogs would treat them as intruders. We named him Banjo, and he was out there alone and unable to leave the property due to our secure fencing. It was a dilemma, and one we could not seem to solve.

All efforts to catch him failed. He was fast. Lisa's son, Brian, and his friends even came with a lasso and tried to catch up with him on the John Deere Gator, our speedy little ATV. No luck. Running on foot was fruitless and climbing over the fence from the road to ambush him was to no avail. We gave up and decided he would stay until he made a decision to be caught. In the meantime, I had to keep him alive.

Every night I strapped on an arm band with a blinking light, and drove the Gator to the bank behind the lake with a bowl of food for Banjo. I proceeded to slowly and precariously slide down the embankment. This was not easy as an unusual amount of rain had made the hill slick, and I grabbed at the vines which slapped me in the face. I did not like the ravine. It smelled of decay and weeds, and the mud was what Kansans call "gumbo." I was spooked at the bottom, had only ventured down there on rare occasions, and never at night. Now I was forced to go down every night because Banjo had to eat.

My husband, Terry, had managed to put a large igloo doghouse full of hay at the bottom of the ravine with the help of the Gator and bungee cords. Terry was in good shape and used to the terrain, but my upbringing had not prepared me for this. However, the demands of living in the country with multiple dogs forced me to learn how to cope in what often seemed like a foreign country.

I put the food in Banjo's house and crawled back up the hill, holding on to tree branches lest I fall backwards. The tangled vines almost made my ascent impossible.

Summer turned into fall, fall into winter. Occasionally we would get glimpses of Banjo but that was all. The food was always gone, and there were occasional sightings of him gliding through the trees like a ghost.

All things come to an end. I always told my daughter when she had a problem that something would tip the scales, and it did for Banjo. One day while I was at school, he changed his pattern and came close to the house. One of our more protective dogs apparently went after him and bit him on his legs. Lisa found some blood on the grass while I was gone, and we knew he had been hurt. My heart sank. I wanted so badly to catch him, hug and comfort him, but he remained out of my reach. I knew we had to find him before infection set in.

For a day or two we caught glimpses of him darting through the trees, but then one day no one saw him at all. That was it. I took off from school, determined to find him. My years of experience warned me he was in trouble.

There was some snow on the ground and patches of ice on the pond, so I dressed in warm clothes and boots and began my search in earnest, cell phone tucked in my pocket. Trekking through the woods and dodging branches, I spotted him lying quietly in a bed of leaves. He did not move, and I feared the worst. Suddenly he heard a rustle, leapt up and raced up the steep embankment at lightening speed. Oh no, how would I catch him? My legs were shaking, and I could hardly hit the numbers on my phone, but I managed to call Lisa for help.

Lisa was on it. She arrived with her daughter, Carolyn, in a matter of minutes. To our alarm, Banjo had managed to scale the steep hill, run across the draw and plunge into the icy waters of our pond, which is really a small lake. He was about 30 feet from the edge and unreachable. His head protruded from the water and there was a thin layer of ice surrounding him. He could move, but he did not. He was immobile and stared at us warily, having mastered the long ago forgotten skills of a dog in the wild. How would we ever get him out?

The catch pole! I had rolled my eyes when Terry ordered a steel catch pole from a catalogue. I knew I would never use it, mainly because I am unable to work anything mechanical. However, Terry mandated we all practice with it in case of an emergency. Two years ago I had waded into the pond and rescued two dogs from the ice, and barely made it back to shore. I really felt I would not be able to do that again without the aid of something like the pole. The one I had denounced as impractical.

But the glorious, magical and beloved catchpole was now our only chance. I ran as fast and hard as I could back to the house, which was fairly far on 50 acres, into the garage and spotted the heavenly apparatus I had ridiculed, hanging patiently on the hook, grabbed it and jumped into the van. I drove, bumping and veering through the pasture toward Lisa and Carolyn whose eyes were riveted on Banjo lest he disappear under the water.

We struggled with the pole. Pushing it toward him, we held the loop precariously over his head, dropped it around his neck, pulled it tight and reeled him in. Once his body was safely on the bank, we could not loosen the wire fast enough, and it was getting too tight. Our hands were shaking, but finally Lisa figured how to release it from around his neck and victory was ours.

I had already called Terry and asked him for help. He left the office early, changed his clothes and came down to the embankment with blankets and towels. We swaddled Banjo securely and managed to load him in the back of the van with Lisa and Carolyn holding him and headed for the emergency clinic.

Banjo was finally ours. This is not how we wanted to capture him, but I had always known on some level that it was going to take a crisis to catch him. Now we were able to look at his face for the first time in eight months. He had been feral, a blur, wild and terrified. Now he was just a dog, he was no longer Cerberus, guarding the gates to hell. He was tired, vulnerable and innocent. He looked up at us, and his face softened as his eyes drifted closed in the warmth of the van and the security of the blankets. What a darling dog! He had such beautiful coloring and a precious face. He had to live, we just could not lose him. It would be unbearable. All these months, all the effort could not be in vain.

The vet's careful examination revealed he had multiple wounds which had become infected and he was dehydrated. She looked at us kindly and said she felt he should be moved to Kansas State Veterinary Hospital where he could receive around the clock care which he desperately needed. Will he live, I asked her? Will he live?

Banjo did live. But it was a long, hard fight. Due to his prolonged exposure to the dirt, pond water and droppings from wildlife in the woods, he had multiple bacterial infections. Finding the right antibiotics was crucial and skin grafts were an ominous possibility, but Banjo was a fighter.

The cash register kept dinging and dinging, but he was hanging in there. Terry said that he would find a way to keep paying his bill after what Banjo had been through. We fought along with him, and the team of vet students were his most ardent cheerleaders. He was a fixture at the hospital, and we became known as "Banjo's parents."

Then a reprieve came. Two vet students called me and said they would bring him home and take care of him daily. This was the answer to a prayer. The bills would slow down, he would be in a home environment and have time to heal physically and emotionally. We all breathed a sigh of relief.

There were some scares along the way. The students had to rush him to the hospital one night when a wound opened. It healed once again and time became his ally, as did his loving personality and beautiful face.

Life has a way of working things out if one is patient and trusting. A vet student who was visiting her friends met Banjo and fell in love. She talked to her fiancé, and they made a decision. Banjo would finally have a home, a safe place to grow old.

We have not heard from the family in a while. Several springs have come and gone since Banjo was first spotted in the distance, gliding through the pasture. We have been told he has never ventured far from their property, knowing inherently that the grass is not always greener on the other side of the pasture fence.

I'll be Home for Christmas

The reason I remember that bleak December morning was because of Fred. It had snowed the night before which had turned into sleet by morning. Due to the weather, I didn't have school that day so I stayed home from teaching, but my husband headed out as always at daybreak.

I was startled when the phone rang a few minutes later. "There's a white pitbull tied to our gate," Terry said, "and it looks like he's had a pretty rough time. I'll run him back to the barn and put him in a pen and head back to work. This dog is going to need our help."

I put on my usual several layers of clothing, heavy boots, and headed out to an adjoining building which was part of our licensed shelter for abandoned dogs. It was furnished with Kuranda beds which are raised off the floor and similar to Army cots. The dogs all loved them, from the Chiuahuas to the St. Bernards.

Terry had left the light on, and when I opened the door it was very quiet. Over in the corner, lying on his bed, was a white dog. I could see the outline of his ribs and his black eyes looked at me guardedly. Even though I have been in animal welfare for 30 years, in addition to my teaching high school English, I was stunned every time I saw a starving animal, and I had seen my share of them. But this one... this one, was haunting. He was dirty and every rib showed, but the worst part was one-third of his backside was blistered and bleeding from what I would find out were acetone burns.

In order to make them mean and aggressive, pit bulls selected to fight are subjected to all kinds of torture. While the crowd cheers, two animals tear each other to shreds for the almighty dollar. Although dog fighting is illegal, the matches continue in basements and isolated areas, in spite of efforts by law enforcement to end this atrocity. The fights end in death for the lucky ones, suffering beyond measure for the less fortunate.

Fred had clearly failed, but how had he come to be chained to our gate with a tattered, wet bag of cheap dog food lying in the snow, I would never find out. Many of us had our theories. We all suspected someone had rescued him and brought him to us, unable to witness his pain any longer.

And so Fred came to SCARS

The room was warm, and I had left the radio on the night before. KMAJ radio was playing "I'll be Home for Christmas." I knelt down quietly beside him and saw that look that I had seen far too many times, "What did I do? Did I do something wrong?" I looked in his eyes and said, "You did nothing wrong, you just fell into the wrong hands, but you're safe now... you're safe."

With Christmas around the corner, I was busy decorating upstairs in the room reserved only for humans…no furry creatures allowed. Maybe it was time to make an exception. So, Fred spent his evenings nestled under the tree while I wrapped presents. He slept deeply. Every now and then he would open his eyes, watch me and drift off again. He knew he was safe at last and, oh, how I loved this dog.

Christmas came and went and finally spring arrived with wild flowers blooming in the pasture. Fred began playing with the other dogs. One of his favorite pastimes was romping with Winston, our Saint Bernard. They would run in unison, sharing a stick until it broke in two and then run off to the pond together, the broken stick left far behind. Fred also loved sun bathing which posed a problem since he had scar tissue on 1/3 of his back. The vet said hair would never grow back on that area, so we had to be careful in the summer. On hot days we all scrambled around looking for the sun screen. "Don't let Freddie out" was the battle cry until the lotion was found and applied.

One day a friend came by with a woman who claimed to be an "animal communicator." I was somewhat skeptical, but my friend wanted her to meet Fred. She looked at him quietly and said, "I see fire." I closed my eyes. I could not bear to think of what he had endured. She said he had one fear. "He is terrified he might have to leave here." I knew then, as I had known from the beginning, Fred would stay with us until his last days.

Epilogue:

Fred died three years later over Christmas, almost to the day we found him. He had cancer, which may have been brewing for some time. We never knew how old he was, but he was not young. Fred was a priceless gift. He taught us about bravery, love and patience. We will never know how long he waited to be rescued from his hell, but he endured until the day came.

We saved his ashes as a reminder of a light that burned briefly, but brightly, in our lives, and a memorial stone points the way to the lake where he chased sticks and swam so joyfully on the last days of his life.

Blinky's Bucket List

One hot, muggy, summer morning, I noticed something ambling slowly up our quarter mile long gravel driveway toward the house, or lane as Terry calls it. Walking out to the gate, I saw a small white dog, heavily matted, with an eye that was inflamed and protruding. He looked miserable, hot and tired. "Good grief, how did you get here?" I asked, and carried him into the house. On closer inspection, he weighed about 10 pounds, and his left eye was alarming. Actually, the right one did not look too good either, but it was not as critical. We decided someone must have dumped him, unable to pay for his clearly needed surgery.

Off he went to the veterinarian who said the eye had to come out, now. He came through the surgery well and settled into a life of complacency perched on the air conditioning vent in the kitchen. We think he could see some light in his other eye, but for the most part, he was blind. Did we worry about him being blind? Heck no, old Blinky, as we named him, was going nowhere, or so we thought. However, luxuriating on the vent, unbeknownst to us, Blinky was working on his bucket list and dreaming of a life of adventure.

One evening when the temps were over 100, not unusual for a Kansas summer, we could not find Blinky. Now mind you, we have 50 acres, much of which is dense brush and thick trees. I once lost a St. Bernard in five minutes right in front of me. Therefore, I count the dogs all day long, and I panic if one is missing for over 5 minutes. OCD kicks in with a vengeance, and I force anyone and everyone around me into high gear shrieking the dog's name, frightening everyone in the house and on our property. I start racing around looking in every corner, upstairs, downstairs, in every closet and room. Terry tells me to calm down, but it is hopeless. I have to find them fast. I could not find Blinky, and it was getting dark.

Out came the flashlights, and we donned high rubber boots as we feared he had fallen into the pond and drowned. We must have searched for over two hours… nothing…no Blinky. Where was he???

The next day Terry came home early from work, changed his clothes and drained the fish pond. Nothing. We were running out of ideas. We called our next door neighbors, and they came with flashlights. No luck.

For a variety of reasons, the main one being the unpredictable weather, we do not want to lose a dog here at our sanctuary. If one takes off, terror strikes instantly because of the ever present threat of bad weather. I am either frantic about the blistering heat, powerful winds, torrential rain, or blinding snow. Tornadoes, roll clouds, dust storms, straight line winds, and funnel clouds are terms I had never heard back East, but they are real, and they happen in Kansas. My cousin said it perfectly, there is nothing between Canada and Kansas but a barbed wire fence.

To make matters worse, it began to thunder. Terry and I stood on the front porch and looked at the vast, ominous sky. He grew up on a 1500 acre farm in western Kansas; I had never been on a farm. He understood the weather on the land as my father understood it at sea. I remember Dad telling me one time his ship was running from three typhoons in the Sea of Japan. Terry had been on the fringes of two tornadoes.

Terry said, "I don't like the look of those clouds, they are full of rain." I looked at them and saw nothing unusual. "Weatherman says a storm's coming with straight line winds, so make sure all the dogs are inside." I have been here for over 25 years and still do not know what straight line winds are and not sure I want to. They are probably the ones that make the trees lie down flat when I look out the window. That night the wind howled and the rain pounded relentlessly on the windows. Neither of us got any sleep.

Terry particularly loved Blinky, in spite of the fact he growled and showed his sharp little yellow teeth on many occasions. He hated new people and despised dogs bigger than he. We told each other he was nervous, but, in truth, he was just disagreeable.

But the longer he was gone, I thought maybe Terry was right, maybe Blinky wasn't such a bad little guy. Suddenly I remember him being incredibly cute and sweet. I wondered why I had referred to him as Mr. Grumpy most of the time. The more I thought about it, the more I missed him.

On day three, Terry stayed home from work. Where was that little, white, fluffy, blind stinker. If Terry in his determination could not find him, no one could. I had to go to school the next day, as I was starting a new unit in Mythology. Terry, as the president of his firm, could do what he wanted when it wasn't tax season.

During the fifth hour, I was in the middle of a lesson on Odysseus and his adventures sailing home to Ithaca when I noticed some of the students muttering and looking at the door. I turned my head and standing in the doorway of my classroom was my husband, in a rumpled suit, clutching a bedraggled white dog. I put my book down on the podium, walked quickly to the door and out into the hall. Blinky was alive.

Here is what happened. Terry said he stayed home and started walking the pastures, calling Blinky's name. After all, he was blind in one eye, not deaf. He walked and walked, drove around in the Gator and finally had to admit defeat and return to work. He went back to the house, put on his suit, got in the car and headed down the driveway. Looking in both directions, something caught his eye in the south pasture. Near the fence line he saw a shining light like a reflection of a mirror, and he followed it. He had no idea what it was or where it came from. He climbed the fence in his suit, looked down into the ravine and saw what he initially thought was a white rock. Did it move, or was it his imagination? Sliding slowly down the hill, beneath where he had seen the light, he called Blinky's name. The "rock" was our scared, wet and tired little white dog who was attempting to stand. With his hands shaking , Terry gently scooped him up and made his way back up the hill. The light was gone.

For some unknown reason, Blinky had gone out-side, began walking, circled the pond, and kept going. This little dog, in his declining years and mostly blind, covered the greater part of 50 acres in brutal heat, a night of rain and wind, and was lost for the better part of three days. Why he ventured out for the first time in his life, we will never know for sure, but he embarked on an odyssey that must have been on his bucket list. Months of hearing the other dogs talk about the fun walk around the pond gave this little dog big ideas. If they could do it so could he, even though he couldn't see very well.

Blinky came back to the house after his rescue, resumed his sedentary life, and never got it into his head again to go awandering. He wadded up his list and settled back on his favorite air conditioner vent, surrounded by his friends and family. They were pretty nice actually.

Where did the light come from? Where did it go? Another unanswered question, but Blinky knows this: even if your bucket list lures you down a yellow brick road to a magical kingdom, there is really no place like home.

Rock Star

YOU GOTTA COME GIT HER!!! I held the phone away from my ear as "Sue" screeched that her dog, Honey, was an escape artist and kept getting out of the fence. "We can't keep her, the neighbors are threatening me and the landlord is cussing a lot."

This was not a good part of town for a dog to be running loose, so I decided I had better check it out. When I pulled my car up to the curb, Sue came staggering out of her door being dragged by an exuberant dog who was clearly in charge. Honey was extremely thin, but it did not slow her down one bit. Sue fell over into the grass with the dog leaping and twirling while the frayed leash wrapped itself determinedly around her ankles. She was shouting that she could not control Honey, which had become vividly apparent.

I did not want to take this dog, nor did I want to leave her here. About this time, with the owner still wallowing in the yard, my friend and fellow teacher, Lori pulled up. Lori was a faithful volunteer and foster for SCARS, and I had called her knowing she was a sucker for boxers and only real sucker would take this one.

True to form, Lori said "I'll take her!" and somehow managed to extricate the leash from the woman's legs and pile Honey into her car. I did not even bother to have the woman sign the surrender form knowing it would be awhile before she was up and about again. We scurried off leaving her in the dust (literally).

The next day Lori called me shrieking, "Honey is gone! I don't know how she got out of the fence, but there is no sign of her." This was not good as the thermometer had hit over 100 degrees and heat advisories were being announced on TV and radio. "Keep your pets inside," was the shrill reminder, which was hard to do when you could not find your pet.

Teachers are great at making posters, so off Lori went to Staples to make lost signs with Honey's picture and both of our phone numbers. Lori and Jenny, another fellow teacher and volunteer, plastered signs in the general vicinity of Honey's previous "home" thinking she might want to return there, but hoped she was smarter than that. Meanwhile temperatures soared and I was sure she was starving and had collapsed from heat prostration. The three of us bordered on hysteria due to the fact she was skin and bones when we got her.

Days went by and Lori and Jenny kept their vigil, logging an impressive number of miles in areas that it is wise to travel in twos. They actually spotted her dumpster diving on one occasion and before they could grab her, she eluded them and disappeared. Lori said the only way we would ever catch her would be if she ran into a yard, and we trapped her. Good luck with that fantasy.

The following Friday the four of us met at our favorite restaurant. Terry was starting to relax after a long day of figuring out "impossible taxes from clients who had forgotten to bring vital forms," with the help of a muy fuerte marguerita. Then Lori's cell phone rang from someone who had seen her number on the poster. She answered it, "Are you sure it is a tan boxer? You better be sure, because I am having way more fun here than I will be chasing this blasted dog." Yes, it was a tan boxer and this was day nine and she was still alive in this brutal heat?

We looked at each other, jumped out of our seats, grabbed the keys sitting on the table to Terry's new car, and ran out with him just raising the drink to his mouth. "We'll be back," I promised as we flew out the door.

Zipping around behind Topeka High School, our rival school of all the nerve, we spotted Honey. She leapt across an incredibly high cement wall and disappeared. Good grief that was quite a feat. We suddenly spotted two men leaning against a telephone pole who slurred loudly and pointed, "THAT WAY!!!"

Around the corner again, tires peeling, we saw Honey dart into a yard of an abandoned house. WOOHOO!!! We could get her now. I slammed on the brakes, and left the Terry's shiny new car idling in the middle of the road (I am really glad he did not see that) while Jenny and Lori sprinted into the yard on foot. We slammed the gate behind us, trapping her inside. Oh no, Lori would be bragging for months about her prediction being right on target.

Honey darted onto the back porch and sat there jubilantly while we embraced her, despite the fact she was filthy and smelly. Visions of her, emaciated and staggering around in the heat had danced in my head for days. We all looked at each other, Honey had gained weight.

We loaded her into the car, and headed back to the restaurant where Terry had given up and dozed off at the table, still in a sitting position.

And so Honey came to live at SCARS…

Once here, Honey took charge. She never once tried to escape, but she developed her own entertainment. Leaping into the air catching dragonflies in the summer took the place of finding holes in a fence.

She has also found another means to entertain herself: rock carrying. Picking up huge rocks daily that are bigger than her head, she staggers around the pastures. Onlookers are stunned when they see her zig zagging around with a boulder in her mouth.

In spite of her idiosyncrasies, everyone loves her. When our friend's two daughters spend the night here, Honey sprawls across the bed in ecstasy, tail wagging every minute. But for some reason, she has never been adopted. We often wonder if her compulsion to dig up and carry rocks around puts people off.

So, in the meantime, we continue to twist our ankles as we walk around the pasture stepping in huge holes once filled by rocks of varying sizes. Honey blames them on the gophers. We know better.

A Place Called SCARS

Mother and Teddy

Into the Rain

Two chihuahuas were in trouble. They lived at a house with questionable "comings and goings" in the night, and rumors abounded about the activities inside. Kelli, our faithful volunteer, was visiting a friend who lived near there, and the girls decided to walk down the street and "check things out." Sure enough, there were two tiny dogs in the yard, and they looked thin, dirty, frightened and hopeless. Feeling bold, Kelli walked up to the door and knocked, hoping the owners of the dogs would give them away. A man opened the door. His reply when she asked if they could have the puppies was "Take the rats," and our little foursome disappeared into the night air.

And so Lulu and Coco came to SCARS.

The staff here refers to Kelli as the "dog whisperer." At a whopping eighty pounds, there is no dog she cannot handle, no dog that does not love her, no dog she cannot train. She can groom, clean ears, brush, bathe and medicate any dog regardless of their size. Kelli is relentless in examining every orifice. No yeasty ear escapes her scrutiny and hearing "Do you have any more Q tips? Where are the Baytril ear drops? The medicated shampoo?" are all too familiar queries around here. If I had a nickel for every time someone on our staff has said "I wish Kelli were here," I would be a millionaire.

True to form, no one but Kelli could get near these new chihuahuas, and the two little dogs clung to each other in fear of their lives. Weeks and months went by, and there was little change. They allowed me to feed them, that was all. If anyone else entered the room, the dogs would erupt into blood curdling shrieks. We dubbed them the "harpies," reminiscent of the Greek mythology creatures who swooped down on Phineas daily, tormenting him.

Kelli adored them. We loved Kelli. So, we kept them and waited.

One day an odd thing happened. A retired couple came to look at our dogs, and saw Coco. The wife adored her and by some miracle, Coco seemed to like the woman. Coco sat quietly on her lap while we all looked on in amazement. Her big brown eyes and fluffy body were irresistible. Lulu, on the other hand, was being her usual antagonistic, unfriendly self. Her short haired, brindle coat could not compete with Coco. When anyone approached her, she would show her little needle teeth, so that usually ended any interest in her. The couple wanted to give Coco a try at their home.

We decided perhaps Coco and Lulu would be better behaved if they were separated, and Coco headed for their lake house in Emporia, Kansas, dressed in a little blue halter with a SCARS tag. The car door opened when they got home, and Coco bolted into the woods and disappeared in the rain.

We all launched into action, posting flyers and making phone calls, but the weather was not on our side. It had been raining non-stop for eight days. The lake was high, and the trees were dripping with water, the mud getting worse and worse. The flyers fell off of the trees, leaving nails with only shreds of paper left. Wet signs lay on the ground with the word "LOST" barely discernable in the streaking colors.

She was out there somewhere, but we could not find her. How could a six pound chihuahua survive alone in this weather? Petitions to heaven were going up in record numbers for this tiny, vulnerable creature once again in peril.

Kelli was inconsolable. She adored Coco and had saved her, now this. Kelli, at age 30, had been diagnosed with cancer and was facing major surgery in a few weeks. This would be followed by at least a year of chemotherapy and radiation. Her bond was so powerful with these two little dogs that all of us felt if Kelli was going to beat this, she had to find Coco. And we needed a plan.

Feeling not a minute could be lost, Kelli and her mom planned to drive the hour trip from Topeka to Emporia every single day. There was no time to lose, as the coyotes howled ominously at night.

Kelli and Sue canvassed the neighborhood and gave flyers to everyone living around the lake. Knowing pictures get people's attention, they posted them on telephone poles and trees. Everyone was worried and promised to watch for her. My number was posted, as was Kelli's, and we waited.

Three days later, I got a call from a neighbor. She spotted a small brown animal drinking from the lake wearing "something blue." My heart leaped. I called Kelli, gave her the woman's number, and she headed to Emporia. There was no sign of Coco and no other sightings. She had vanished once again.

It was time for desperate measures. A seven pound brindle chihuahua, Lulu, was Coco's sidekick and best friend. If anyone could lure her out, it was Lulu. Dressed in a blue raincoat and a halter, she was now a search and rescue dog.

Kelli and Lulu walked for miles and miles, trudging through the woods and rain, calling for Coco. It got darker and as night fell, Kelli got out her flashlight. Finally, she gave up, as Lulu's strength was faltering. They were soaked and shivering. Turning up the heat and heading home, they were defeated once again.

On day eight, we had all about given up hope. But then my phone rang. It sounded like an older man, "I think we have your dog in our yard." Could it possibly be her? Could she have survived for so long in this weather with no food? He said she was lying on the edge of the yard, far from the house and not moving. "Do not go near her," I warned him, "She is terrified of people and might take off again."

Kelli was there in one hour. She knew what to do….get on her stomach, crawl slowly towards Coco gently calling her name. She may be feral by now, we had been warned, so be careful. In spite of her prolonged isolation and trauma, Coco had not forgotten her rescuer.

When Kelli crawled toward her, Coco stood up and staggered in her direction. She was going home at last.

The three of us met at the veterinary clinic. Coco had a fever of 108 and was in shock, but she was alive. The vet found a thorn embedded in her armpit, which the halter held in place. Unable to run without pain, she was finally forced to stop her endless roaming.

Coco got well in time, Kelli is recovering from surgery and a tough year of chemotherapy and radiation. Coco and Lulu live here now, and Kelli comes to see them every week. A tiny army bound together by the will to survive.

A Pit Bull, a Raccoon, and a Commercial Washing Machine

"Don't make any sharp turns," my husband sternly warned me from the passenger seat of his truck. I looked back warily at the large commercial washing machine leaning somewhat precariously in the back of the truck as we sped along I70 from Abilene to Topeka.

The clouds were scudding and turning steel gray as evening approached. If we kept up this pace, we would be home to take care of our 50+ dogs before dark. This machine was one more effort to keep up with the crushing demands of running a dog rescue. The two washing machines at home ran continuously and had to be replaced every year or two. Terry decided it was time to get serious and invest in a commercial washer which was now in the back of our truck.

The weather in Kansas is intimidating, to say the least, which increased my concern about a pit bull in the back yard of a run down house not far from us. A friend of mine, Janie, kept her horses in a pasture behind the house where the pit bull lived, or rather existed, and kept me apprised of her condition. Mama Pittie, as we called her, had a tumor the size of a basketball on her side, and it continued to grow in the apparent absence of medical care.

Mama had survived the summer because Janie was feeding her when she could, and she had access to water from the pond, but fall was approaching with winter close behind which created a new set of problems. To make things worse, Janie said the dog had already delivered multiple litters and suspected another was on the way. She said many of her pups had died, so I hoped she was not pregnant again.

I was wrong.

As I teetered along I 70, with my steel passenger rocking in the back of the truck, my cell phone kept ringing. I peeked at my husband who was napping and quietly answered my phone. Uh oh, it was my friend, Denise, who was also worried about mama dog. She said, "Janie just called me screaming and crying that mama dog had been attacked by a raccoon right in front of her while she was feeding her horses, and there was blood everywhere, and then Janie's phone went dead. I think she passed out." This was catastrophic and here I was driving in the fast approaching dark with the washing machine rocking in the back. How was I going to rescue a dog in this situation? I begged Denise to drive to the house where mama may be dying. There was no time to lose!

I knew it would take Denise awhile to get across town, so by the time we turned off of I 70 onto our exit, I was devising a plan which included a turn, maybe two, on a gravel road. That was forbidden due to the cumbersome passenger in the bed of the truck, but I had to convince Terry to let me make a slight detour. I carefully broached the subject of the struggle between mama pittie and the racoon, and feared she would be the loser. Could I make a TINY turn on to the country road where she lived...PLEASE!!

Terry, being understanding when it comes to dogs said, yes, if I was extremely careful. With that green light, I headed in terror down the dirt road, turned at an agonizingly slow pace and found the house in a quarter of a mile. I peered out of the window, straining my eyes, but the dim porch light cast only a faint glow onto the ominously still yard. Nothing moved, nothing. I headed home with a heavy heart.

When I pulled into our driveway, Terry got the dolly so he could move the monstrosity into the garage. I let all 50 dogs out of the house and checked my phone. Still no word from Janie who had probably passed out, fallen in the creek and drowned next to the dead mama dog with the raccoon marching proudly away.

Then I heard a tiny ping, and looked at my text. It was from Denise. "I got her." I have never read more beautiful words. She then said, "I am on my way to your house." Mind you, Daniel Boone could not have found our house at night, but Denise persevered, and I soon saw her head lights heading down our long gravel driveway.

As she slowed to a stop, I shined my flashlight in the car. Next to her was mama dog, her face bleeding, her eye swollen, but she was alive and nestled in the blanket on the passenger seat.

I exhaled for the first time in hours.

Denise said "I just went up to the door and when the owner answered, I told him his dog would not make it through the night without medical help, and I would be willing to take her to the emergency vet right now and pay the bill." She admitted throwing in the possibility of rabies which brings to mind horrible memories of Old Yeller dying a painful death and humans getting shots straight into their stomachs.

After months of begging the authorities to intervene on the dog's behalf, Mr. Raccoon gave us the window we needed, and mama was on her way to safety. Sadly, Mr. Raccoon met his demise at the wrath of a tough little pit bull. But we are forever in his debt.

Denise decided to head for the veterinary emergency clinic immediately, but she had forgotten her wallet. I didn't have any cash, and by this time Terry was asleep in bed. This was serious, all I could do was get the donation jar full of change out of my car and give it to her. "I am NOT using donations, she wailed, but I insisted saying it was for mama pittie. Off she went with an battered dog next to her, and a jingling jar in the back seat of her car.

Here is what happened. The vet examined mama, stapled the wounds on her face and feet, took blood and found she was heartworm positive, Ehrlichia positive and would have babies any day. In addition, the tumor on her side was going to make her delivery uncomfortable, but she was a farm dog and her litters numbered in the hundreds. Well, maybe not that many, but close. It was precarious, but this gal was tough.

The rest of the story......

The vet was right. Mama settled into her new digs here in the Morton Building and one night, (it could not be during the day) she began to deliver her next litter. My friend, Jenny, hung in there with me. On number eight I threw up my hands and went into the house to rethink the wisdom of having become immersed in dog rescue. Jenny valiantly remained as her midwife, and said she would text me when the next puppy arrived. No sooner had I gotten into the house that phone dinged "number nine!" Visions of tiny puppies scurrying around eating and pooping, and repeating this ritual for weeks, maybe months danced in my now exhausted brain. In addition, I could hear the cash register running up the bills for shots, worming, puppy food and a million other things. I ran back to the Morton Building and Jenny screeched "number ten!!" I said, "That's it, mama, you are done!" She ignored me and popped out number eleven.

Now she was done.

The following weeks, while the pups ate and grew, we humans staggered around in a daze. After all, there were 50 other dogs to care for with their own set of problems. Never mind, we marched on and declared mama to get an eleven on a scale of ten for best mommy in the world. She adored them and we promised her we would not let this litter die. She fed and cuddled them endlessly and protected them from all foreign invaders, human and canine. And they thrived.

But the story is not over yet...

The tumor that resembled a large basketball is now history. She was taken to the vet for a biopsy and evaluation, and the egregious growth was a large fatty tumor which could be removed. Mama sailed through the surgery with her usual aplomb, and regained her once girlish figure. Despite her now attractive appearance, she was also spayed so her days of being a siren are over. That seems to be fine with her as we notice she passes out on the sofa quite early these days.

Her eleven pups are safely adopted and settled in their forever homes, so mama can finally put the tough days behind her, and look forward to a peaceful passing of her youth.

The Paper Bag Dog

Auburn is a small rural town which lies about ten miles south of Topeka, Kansas, the state capital. Some would refer to it as a borough, but the inhabitants choose to call it a town, although there is not even a traffic light to give it notability.

The town does boast a gas station which everyone calls the Gas Depot, although it was bought out by some big company and given a fancy name no one can remember. There is an elementary school, a community center, two churches and a few local businesses.

Every Tuesday from Memorial Day to Labor Day, the locals bring their goods to the Farmer's Market and set up little wobbly tables in the church parking lot, sell potatoes, corn, beans and home baked desserts that are delicious, but verboten for diabetics. Paper signs mark the prices, but they are often negotiable as the day wanes.

Behind the church are some modest houses and beyond them a nursing home with a pond. A duck named Henry once lived on that pond, and the "dog rescue Lady" (that would be me) was called to rescue and move him as some of the crankier inhabitants resented his squawking at odd hours. With the help of my "bird

71

friends," Henry was relocated to a more tolerant environment.

Among the residents living in modest houses behind the gas depot was Rebecca Albertson. She was thought of by the natives as "odd" or "different." She was a pleasant woman in her mid-fifties and retired. She owned her house and had a medium sized dog named Muffin, a scruffy looking creature whom she walked daily. However, she was from "back east" and not a native of Auburn. Thus she remained permanently an outsider. To her credit, when she spotted a little blonde stray dog running loose for several days, maybe weeks, she took the initiative to get out her phone book (yes, they do still exist) and began looking up dog rescues.

One would think that most of the town would be aware of a licensed dog rescue five miles on the outskirts of Auburn on 50 acres but, surprisingly, not everyone knows about SCARS. The entire states of Kansas and Missouri sure know who we are, but the little town of Auburn remains blissfully unaware of the "famous" people outside of town who were written up in a national magazine and on the cover of the local newspaper. I doubt they would be impressed, being more concerned about gas prices and wheat needing to be harvested.

We do have our name and number in the yellow pages as dictated by the state, but beyond that we choose to remain somewhat anonymous for obvious reasons. One reason being the desire to be warned when new dogs arrive, rather than finding them tied to our gate or loose on the property and fleeing from a herd of resident dogs.

So ,when the phone rang and Rebecca introduced herself, I was somewhat surprised. She went on the explain that she had seen a small yellow dog running around Auburn and was leaving food out for it every night. She was not able to get close to it, and when she spoke with the people in the house where the dog hid out, they seemed unconcerned.

When she called me, the temperatures had been over 100 for three days. I was trying to think where the dog might find a source of water other than Henry's pond, which would be adequate but she might not be able to find it. In the meantime, Rebecca and I agreed she must be caught. (I referred to her as a she but did not know that for sure!)

Bridget and Patrick are youngsters, in my opinion, and work here at SCARS. I told them the situation and they found and set up the live trap in our garage that I had not seen in years. They practiced how to use the trap door, loaded it in the car and drove down the driveway with a bag of hot dogs squashed in Bridget's purse. With Rebecca's address and instructions to go to her house, she would show them where the dog was last seen. I went back to my chores and waited for them to either call or text me.

An hour later, I saw the car coming back down our long driveway and peered hopefully over the fence to see if they had a dog with them. No dog. Bridget came up to me in her usual breathless voice and stated loudly, "Rebecca is a NUT CASE!!" Patrick hustled up next to her and said, "Rebecca is PSYCHO!" Having been a high school teacher for decades, I know teenagers have a propensity for hyperbole, but really? Rebecca sounded perfectly normal to me on the phone. But then, I am also an Easterner, which makes me questionable. Aren't I the one who thought bread was born in a plastic bag?

The kids went on to tell me that Rebecca dragged them up and down the road looking for the dog, and then was jubilantly jumping up and down pointing at the "little blonde dog" who was not moving in front of some bushes. She must be hurt or sick! The kids were lying on the grass and trying to sneak up on the dog, but it refused to move. Rebecca stood behind them biting her nails. Suddenly a breeze came up and the "dog" was lifted into the air and sailed across the lawn. It was a paper bag.

Rebecca called again the next day and said she knew we all thought she was nuts, but the dog was in the yard again, and this time, it was not a paper bag. She lamented having forgotten her glasses the last time she called.

Patrick and Bridget got reluctantly into the car again, not bothering to load up the trap this time. An hour passed and once again I saw the car coming back down our driveway, but now it had a third passenger. Sitting fixedly in the seat next to them was a darling little blonde dog, probably a Cairn terrier mix of some sort. She did not look good. Her breathing was rapid and her eyes glassy.

Since my social life consists of daily visits to the vet, I called the clinic and warned them I was on my way with an emergency.

Our little stray had a fever of 104 and was gasping for breath. The vet said to leave her there, they would do a battery of tests to determine what was going on. Several hours later, I returned to see our charge on IV fluids, and they were injecting her with a syringe of Vitamin K that would have scared an elephant.

Turning to look at me, the vet said the X rays showed a collapsed trachea, and her entire chest cavity was filled with blood. They could barely control the bleeding from a blood test. Apparently she had ingested a large amount of rat poison during her adventures. The outcome was dubious, and the fight to save her was on.

I kissed her goodbye, left the clinic and got disconsolately into my car. Why was this always happening to me? Too many dogs come to us on their last leg, so to speak, and we have to save them at an enormous emotional and financial cost. I put my head on the steering wheel. I was chronically tired, worried and physically exhausted. Retirement from teaching had not brought the relaxation I had dreamed of, and many days I wished I were back in school.

And to make matters more stressful, Rebecca called me continually with questions about this dog. Was she ok? Would she live? Can I go visit her? Of course, I did not know if she would make it or not, and I told her the vet was not encouraging. She would then commence crying that she had waited too long to find help. I tried to console her, but I felt miserable too.

That night I tossed and turned, trying to prepare myself for the worst. In the morning, I watched the clock.

7:45, 7:50,7:55,8:00. I dialed the all too familiar number and held my breath.

"Hi, this is Maureen, and I am calling about the little dog I brought in yesterday." I am sure she waited at least an hour to respond, but when she did, I exhaled. "She is doing really well, better than we had expected. We just walked her and she pottied and came right back in and settled down." I was ecstatic.

This dog was a survivor for sure. The vet warned me somberly that she had two weeks before we could be sure she would survive. He said she had to stay there for two more days, and then I could take her home. Oh yes! He forgot to tell me she was microchipped and wrote down the address of the owner. The dog's name was registered as Katydid.

I looked at the clock and decided I had time to take a drive into the country and find the owner. Navigating my way around gravel roads, without the help of street signs, I finally pulled up to a house that matched the address on the microchip. It was a brick rancher, old and in disrepair. The windows were open and the torn curtains billowed out in the breeze.

I walked up to the door and knocked, but no one answered, so I strolled around to the side and heard a woman talking to someone. I stopped and felt like a voyeur, but I actually looked in the open window and saw her talking animatedly on the phone. I called to her quite loudly and she did not hear me, so I really screamed out loud, HELLO!!!! Finally, she turned and looked past the faded curtains, and put the phone down and got up.

"Fran" and her boxer came rushing out of the back door onto the porch strewn with old toys, shoes, tennis balls and dead potted plants. She greeted me amicably and I broached the subject of her errant dog. Her face sort of crinkled up and she looked a bit skeptical. "You found Katydid?" I told her how I had come to have her dog in my possession, or rather in the clinic, and she seemed genuinely concerned BUT she did say that Katy and Boo-boo did not get along well, and life had been calmer with Katy gone.

She informed me that six weeks ago she and her two dogs were at the infamous gas depot getting gas for her car when Katydid proceeded to leap out of the window and race across the street and disappear behind the elementary school. Fran jumped back in the car in hot pursuit, but Katy was nowhere to be seen. She drove around for a while and finally went home. No posters, no lost ads, but she did call the local vet to inform them that Katydid was now on the lam. Katy was on her own.

I assured her we would take good care of Katy, and Fran signed a form surrendering her to SCARS, and I was on my way. She wanted me to keep her up dated on news of Katy, which I promised to do, but probably would not. I left with her smiling gayly as Booboo chased my car down the driveway, biting at the tires.

From then on it was smooth sailing. Katy was released from the clinic, I was given a bottle of Vitamin K pills to administer for three weeks, and she would be good to go.

Katy was adorable. She sat up on her hind legs and put her little front feet up when she wanted a treat.

She ran happily to the pond with our crew, slept in our bedroom and never had an accident. She had a group of followers on Facebook who were cheering on her with "Katy did it!!" I posted pictures daily… she had become a star!

We put her on our website, and waited for the PERFECT home, which actually does exist, because she got one. A wonderful young woman saw her picture, read her story, filled out an application and headed for Kansas from Norwalk, Iowa. Mary, her new owner, was single and the two of them would be a fabulous team.

It was love at first sight. I had warned her that Katy bolted from cars and Mary was on it. She had purchased a harness for the back seat so Katy would be safe. Mary was prepared with everything Katy could ever need, and most of all, she had enough love to last Katy for the rest of her life.

As the car pulled away and down our gravel driveway, my eyes blurred. I had feared she would die, and she lived. The concerned neighbor found help, the vet fought for her, SCARS fought for her, Facebook friends encouraged and cheered her on and she did it, Katy did it.

A Field of Daisies

I try to live an honest life and not break the law, but I felt slightly nervous when I saw the name on the caller ID: Sheriff. I remembered breaking the speed limit, just a tad, the last time I was in that county, but after all it is in the middle of nowhere and I hadn't seen any police cars hiding in the trees. The dispatcher said Sheriff Morrison wanted to speak to me and to hold on for a minute. This was torture.

Fortunately, she got straight to the point, "There are two dogs in Waynesville who need to get out of their present situation ASAP. Can your shelter take them?" While I always dread hearing about suffering dogs, I was thankful I would not be wearing an orange suit any time soon. "Of course, we will take them."

Sheriff Morrison set up a time for me to come to the central office. I have learned it is best not to go alone on a dog rescue, so I called my friend and volunteer, Jenny. She was always ready and willing to help as long as she wasn't teaching a class or coaching the girls' softball team.

Arriving at the sheriff's department, we were introduced to two police officers who were waiting for us. This was getting serious. However, Jenny looked over at me and said that one of the officers had been in her math class in high school. "Did he pass?" I asked? She nodded yes, so I breathed a sigh of relief.

With a police car in front of us and behind us, we drove fifteen miles through the county and finally saw a small faded sign: Waynesville. I had been there once before and nothing had improved. The town consisted primarily of rusted mobile homes, many were missing windows and doors. Although a few people still lived in the town, there was not a store or gas station. Most of the residents had moved out.

We found out there were three dogs who needed immediate help; a boxer, a shepherd mix and a blonde lab puppy. Although we came to love them all, this story is mainly about Hope. She won my heart from the minute I saw her crumpled on the ground, unable to stand.

I have learned the hard way that alienating an abusive owner only hurts the dog. The owners become defensive, throw us off the property, and the dogs disappear. I cannot help an animal if I do not get it surrendered, and rescuing a starving, mistreated dog is my number one goal. Owners can be dealt with later, but getting the dog is always my first priority.

The man who lived in the house marched out with a belligerent look on his face. He was stocky, wore blue jeans and had confederate flags tattooed on his arms. A cigarette bounced up and down in his mouth as he gruffly spoke to us. He had apparently agreed to turn over the dogs to a rescue and SCARS was chosen. I avoided looking at him as we walked over to the side yard. There was no grass, only dirt, broken toys, bottles and two dogs, a Boxer and a German shepherd mix.

The Boxer was down, groveling under the fence trying to reach something. The man laughed derisively while she tried to get at the neighbor's chickens, desperate for food. She was crippled, a bag of bones, and covered in mange. She could not get up and had clearly produced too many litters of pups. My heart was pounding, but I said nothing. I looked at Jenny and she averted her eyes. Next to the Boxer was a gray female shepherd mix. Her back was sunken, every rib protruded, but she was able to stand. Her eyes looked at me sad and pleading. How many times had I seen that penetrating look, void of hope.

One of the police officers came out of the house and pulled me aside. He had found a flea infested puppy smelling of feces and urine in a cardboard box. Could we take him too?

Jenny and I waited outside in silence while the police talked to the two owners. Voices were raised. I held my breath. We waited…and waited. Suddenly, the officer waved to me and Jenny and told us to get the dogs into our van. We walked quickly to the yard, Jenny picked up the shepherd, and I picked up the boxer who was heavier than I expected, and I struggled not to drop her. The boxer smelled and her hairless body was black and slippery from mange. She had saggy jowls, bones protruding, crooked paralyzed back legs, a smushed face and I thought she was the most beautiful dog I had ever seen. I held her tightly to me, Jenny kissed the shepherd as she loaded her into the van and the officer went to get the puppy. He was darling, blonde with brown, worried eyes, and his stomach was bloated to the point of bursting; clearly engorged with worms and parasites.

Jenny and I thanked the officers profusely, closed and locked the doors, and drove away as fast as we legally could from the nightmare world that these dogs inhabited.

On the way home we spotted a Dollar Store, and Jenny suggested we stop and grab a bag of dog food. She jumped out and was back in minutes. As she opened the door the Boxer threw herself against the bag and began ripping and tearing it apart. Within seconds all three dogs were devouring the food desperately. We kept driving listening to them eating ravenously. By the time we got home, they were all asleep.

And so Hope, Faith and Puppy came to SCARS…

We have two heated/air conditioned buildings: Bomwell Hall and the Morton building. They each have individual runs with Kuranda beds, which was a luxury for these three. The next step was to make a vet appointment.

Dr. Smith had me haul the boxer, now named Hope, onto the examining table. He listened to her heart, put down his stethoscope, looked directly at me and said, "I don't even know where to begin." Her back legs were paralyzed, she was heartworm positive, she had mange, and was malnourished. One step at a time, I reminded myself over and over.

Faith, the shepherd, could at least walk, but she too was starving, heartworm positive and severely anemic.

The pup's main problem was a massive worm infestation which would take two months to eradicate.

We laid out a plan for them. They needed nourishment, first and foremost. We also treated them for worms and parasites. In the meantime, Dr. Smith recommended we take Hope to Kansas State University Veterinary Hospital where she quickly became a favorite. Her funny smashed nose, large upper body, shrunken hind quarters and lack of hair rendered her irresistible. She was spread out like a Playboy centerfold on the metal table while she was examined.

Hope would never walk again, but with the use of a doggie wheelchair, she could be mobile. Terry did some research and found one for $500 he thought would work. The vets had no other solution to offer, and we all hoped for a miracle.

She accepted her gift graciously and seemed to enjoy the freedom to play with the other dogs, but her front legs tired easily having to do the bulk of the work, and, in time her wheelchair was retired to the basement. It has since been shared with other handicapped dogs.

Considering one of many suggestions, we tried water therapy in our swimming pool. It was a disaster. Hope was terrified and she almost drowned both of us. Then Jenny asked her friend who was a physical therapist for help. Hope loved the massages which several of us tried to continue. We were making her comfortable and secure, feelings she had never experienced.

Faith did not fare as well, and in spite of food and medicine she passed away from severe anemia. Jenny was broken hearted as she had loved her from the moment she gently lifted her into the van and kissed her.

Hope stayed on at SCARS, happy and loved. Her days were busy with the other dogs and visitors, and I loved dressing her up for holidays. She stoically endured the pumpkin outfit, was not thrilled about being an elf for Christmas and wore multiple strands of colored beads for Mardi Gras. She fitted into our family well, and slept on the bed after being carried upstairs.

In early summer our north pasture suddenly blooms into a blanket of bright yellow daisies. One of my favorite pastimes was to take her to the field in the back of the Gator, get her out and let her lie in the sun surrounded by the flowers.

Hope lived with us for three years, gained weight and her coat turned golden red. But the former neglect finally caught up with her and she died peacefully one summer day.

I love all the dogs who have shared their lives with us, but there have been a few I cared for so deeply that saying goodbye was particularly heartbreaking. Such was my love for Hope.

Every year when the pasture once again bursts into bloom , I ride up the hill alone in the Gator and remember her dozing peacefully in the sun under a blue, Kansas sky. Surely she was dreaming of running on four strong legs, because Hope knew one thing for sure, there are no wheelchair dogs in heaven.

Death Row Dog

Three days to live. "Euthanasia: July 11" was posted over the door of the dog kennel. I tracked down a shelter employee and asked her if this was true. "Unfortunately we have no choice. 2-3 days." Rocky was hyperactive,and overstimulated and jumped so hard at people he could not be shown on the adoption floor. He had become a liability.

I looked into a small kennel and came face to face with a furry, freckled, 130 pound, "overstimulated," two year old Saint Bernard. Hardly a ferocious predator, but nevertheless deemed unworthy of a home or a future. I stood there thinking about the transitory nature of life and how little of it this dog had left. Three days= 72 hours=4320 minutes—and there I was contemplating things existential and wasting his precious time. But I was about to stop the clock because I was taking this dog home with me.

I loaded him into the car where he leaped and twirled in the back seat. When I turned around he hit my lip so hard it swelled instantly and I tasted blood. Here was another large, energetic and possibly difficult to control dog, but how could one walk away from a young St. Bernard on death row and sleep at night?

And so Rocky came to SCARS.

When we take in large dogs, a certain routine is followed. They are initially housed in one of our three spacious fenced areas, each with an air conditioned/heated barn. This way the dogs can smell each other while the new guy in town is safely enclosed in his own space. The next step is to bring them in the house where they can learn "inside" behavior. This prepares them to be a companion for a family.

A week after Rocky's arrival, Terry brought him in the living room to watch a football game on TV. He was on a leash. I was cleaning up the kitchen when I heard Terry announce, "If you cannot behave, you are going back outside" and he was marched summarily out the door. Rocky had much to learn.

Subsequently, Terry brought him back into the house every evening and continued to work with him and teach him manners. He was calming down in the house, but still hyperactive outside. Having been locked in a cubicle fit for a chihuahua for so long, he was beside himself.

We did not know how Rocky would interact with the other dogs if we let him loose, so he had to be on a leash when out of his yard. I was usually on the other end of that leash, and I often ended up being dragged in the grass.

There are risks when letting a dog out to run for the first time. Lacking previous exercise they could collapse from exhaustion, so we take them out briefly and slowly work up to longer and longer runs. We have been witness to the transformation of many dogs when they are given the opportunity to run, unfettered and free. Lack of exercise is one of the primary reasons dogs end up in shelters from owners who cannot understand why one walk after dinner is not enough. I wasn't sure Rocky was ready, but I was getting tired of washing grass stains out of my clothes.

One evening when the sun was starting to set, leaving a red glow across the pastures, I decided to let Rocky run behind the Gator to the pond. This is an excellent workout and most dogs love chasing after anything with tires. I hit the gas pedal and he followed closely behind, running easily in the high grass. As I neared the big pond, I slowed down and so did he.

Rocky looked around and walked carefully to the edge of the water which sparkled in the waning sunlight, the trees were moving slowly in the breeze and I said "Go on, you can do it!" and he tiptoed into the shallow end and hesitated. Then it was as if a voice only he could hear urged him on, and he slid carefully into the deep waters, paddled around the dock, then turned his head and swam majestically toward the middle of the pond. Those waters were working their magic on memories that we can only imagine and will never fully understand. The loneliness, isolation and despair of the voiceless was ebbing away in the baptismal water as he swam with increasing confidence. Gone was the crushing confinement of cement walls, the deafening, endless howls of the shelter dogs. Then he turned and headed back to me paddling rhythmically. He kept turning and swimming, turning again and again, gracefully and purposely. I watched in fascination as the sun dropped behind the horizon and realized I was now alone in the encroaching darkness with a dog I was just getting to know and possibly could not control.

But that night, dripping wet and loping behind the Gator back to his "room" in our Morton Building, he had been redeemed. After putting him up, I walked into the living room and said to Terry, "I love him. He's going to be okay."

From that night on Rocky and I went to the pond every evening. He was becoming the dog he was born to be before someone had signed his death warrant.

Weeks passed and Rocky's behavior continued to improve. He still jumped too often, got in the "space" of the other dogs, but there was now a flicker of hope--hope that someday he could actually be a family pet. It was up to him.

Someone once told me when we die we will not regret what we have done, but what we have not done. What if I had not allowed Rocky his only chance to live? All I had to say was no, and he would have been silenced forever. There would have been no more hyperactivity, no more jumping, no more swimming. I shuddered at the thought of the power I held. To have this power and not use it humanely would have been unforgiveable.

After a couple of months, the miracle finally happened. I opened an application on my computer, scrolled down and saw the name ROCKY on the line for the desired dog. I thought whoever it was would change their minds once they met him and witnessed his energy level.

But Jessica knew what she wanted. For one thing, she wanted a dog with personality. Rocky fit the bill on that one. He would throw a toy in the air, catch it and run up and down the grass dropping and picking it up. He could entertain himself for hours. And she could not resist his "big ole lovable face."

Jessica and her boyfriend came with their dog for a meet and greet, and the two dogs became fast friends. They ran and chased each other until both were exhausted. Her dog, Copper, was lonely. According to Jessica, he would sit at the fence and whine at the neighbor dogs, yearning to play with them. He needed a buddy.

I showed them where Rocky slept and played so they would be able to duplicate his routine as much as possible. We reviewed the adoption rules, I checked their references, and Rocky lumbered without hesitation into the back seat of their car. Off they went down the driveway with the dust swirling behind them.

I have always contended that there is the right home for every dog, but finding it is not always easy. Dogs have been adopted from here who were blind, deaf, three legged, crippled, overweight, underweight and heretofore unwanted. The human-animal bond is mysterious and inexplicable. In my thirty plus years of working with people and animals, I have never fully understood how or why that moment of intuitive love occurs between a person and a dog, but I am thankful that it does.

Today Rocky's new family sent me a picture of him "shopping" in PetSmart and sitting in front of the toy section. He went home with a basket of new toys that he had chosen himself. "We love him" was written under the picture.

It is bedtime now and the dogs are asleep as I finish this story. Earlier this evening I walked out to the Morton Building to turn off the lights. I automatically looked for Rocky, his blanket was still on the floor and his food bowl was empty. It was quiet and I felt his presence filling the room. What forces had controlled the circumstances surrounding the life of this dog? Where did I fit in?

As Mother Teresa so wisely said, "We can only do small things with great love." It may have been a small thing to have said "Yes, he can come here" but if we were to ask Rocky he would tell you that love was the greatest gift of all.

Urgent~Over Stimulated/humping

EUTH LISTED

KENNEL CM01

#A096573
LAST DAY 7/11

95

MELE

Author's note: *The reasons for surrendering an animal are many and varied. The great majority could be solved by owners taking personal responsibility for their pet. A pet is a lifelong commitment unless the owner cannot give it humane care any longer. Many of the calls I get are for reasons I do not consider acceptable, although we usually take in a dog who needs help unless it has serious behavioral issues.*

In rare instances, an owner surrenders a dog for the right reasons and handles this choice in a responsible manner. Such was Michele's experience, told in her own words.

A New Beginning and When the Time Comes…

There are definitely pitfalls to avoid when taking children shopping at Christmas. At the very tippy top of the list is showing them a black lab puppy with a red bow around her neck in the window of a pet store. If said puppy is also sporting a Santa Claus hat, the parents are doomed. These parents were no exception, so the Christmas present was off to her new home where she was well cared for and lived comfortably for two years. The family had made mistakes: adopting a Black Lab puppy (who could resist) from a pet store at Christmas for the children and there was no fenced yard at their house. They had also done a lot of things right. "Midnight" had been spayed, was up to date on shots and eating expensive dog food. They had a big house in a lovely wooded neighborhood. There was only one thing missing—love. In time the children tired of the dog, the mother had really never wanted a dog and the father traveled. So they did another thing right. They contacted a first rate Lab Rescue, paid a surrender fee, and said their dog was available to an approved home.

I had lost my second Yellow Lab to old age and cancer, and I missed her terribly. Then one morning I woke up and declared my period of mourning over. Life without a dog is not worth living. So for the next month or so, I visited every rescue in Northern Virginia (and on line) and left my phone number and preferences. I was getting further and further afield. One dog turned out to be in Williamsburg, another in Baltimore. I would have adopted Cujo at that point. And then the phone rang: would I be interested in a two year old black female, spayed, owner surrender. I was there in 30 minutes, paid an adoption fee, gave the owner a hug, stuffed the dog in my little car, and zoomed away before anyone had second thoughts.

The first thing we did was to get rid of the name, "Midnight." I thought Mele Kalikimaka suited her. That means Merry Christmas in Hawaii where I spent many happy years and got my first Lab. Mele's days of being ignored were over. No more hiding behind a chair to look invisible. I was working at the time, but I got up early every morning winter and summer to take her to the local dog park where she was everybody's favorite. She slept in my bed. At mid-day she had a dog walker. She had a mobile vet. She went to Halloween parties, visits with Santa, greeted trick or treaters, had a professional portrait done and generally lived life to the fullest. Truth be told, she was having a lot more fun than I was. On occasion I took her to work and the office loved her, but some anonymous sourpuss complained that dogs weren't allowed in the university. They etched a sign on the front door, and I kind of considered it my legacy when I left.

Her favorite day was Saturday when her best friend came to play. Sailor was a young male, a large Yellow Lab, and very boisterous. He ate her food, tore up her toys and knocked her down so hard one day I took her to the vet. But that didn't change anything—she thought he was wonderful. Mele developed cancer when she was twelve, and had a tough last year despite constant visits from the vet. But I had made a deal with her. If she wanted to "hang in there" it was up to her… I would be there for the long haul. Early one Sunday morning I heard some noise in the bathroom where she had taken to sleeping because the floor was cool. I raced in. She had tried to get up a couple of times and then laid back down for the last time. I put my arms around her and kissed her goodbye. We had fought the good fight, but it was over. I was with her, she was at home, she didn't suffer, and she had reached her 13th birthday. That was all I ever asked.

But the Grim Reaper is not an equal opportunity employer; it is finally our responsibility. Some of us do a better job than others when faced with the final decision. In spite of the fact that my sister and her husband have many, many dogs, they treat each one like an only child. But their goal is forever homes, knowing that dogs are happiest when they are part of a family. Over the years SCARS has placed 1,000 dogs in approved homes. Each adoption is captured on their web page under Success Stories.

Years ago, Terry (my brother-in-law) was giving their old rescued Lab an IV drip (hanging from a curtain rod) as the dog lay dying on the couch under a blanket. And in the middle of a Kansas blizzard with all the country roads impassable, the IV bags ran dry. Not to be thwarted, Terry saddled up his tractor, and drove all the way into town to the emergency vet to procure more bags of fluid.

At the other end of the spectrum is the owner who tapes his Boxer's mouth shut and throws him in a ditch to suffer and die. This, alas, is not an isolated case—it happens all the time according to the news. And all along the continuum are lily-livered excuses for dumping an old dog in an already overcrowded pound: he got too big, we have a new baby, divorce, killed a chicken, had an accident and so on ad nauseum. Or the most cowardly act of all—moving out of town and leaving the dog behind in the fenced back yard wondering when someone is coming back for him.

When I was on my dog search I stopped by the county shelter and there was a man with a small dog and a crate and a young child. The dog had to go—his wife was allergic. The little boy had his fingers in the crate saying "Bye Fluffy." That was about ten years ago and I'm still kicking myself for my silence. I've thought of many retorts since then and wondered about the fate of the little dog…and the little boy.

My current dog is a sturdy little Bulldog mix (a rescue from my sister's sanctuary in Kansas) who is aging before my eyes. She has diabetes and gets two shots a day. I think she is mostly blind. Living alone as I do, she is my constant companion and confidante. Perfectly housebroken, she has never seen a crate. But, much to my surprise, last week she went into the guest room and urinated twice on my brand new white shag rug. I guess I'd better throw her in the car and drive her to the local pound. I'm sure a lot of folks would adopt an 11-year-old mixed breed whose insulin costs $179 a month and has cataracts.

No, "when the time comes," I will track down my mobile vet, I will hold Pippa and talk to her and cry an ocean of tears—but I will have done the right thing. And then I'll throw away that rug.

Pippa Goes to Washington

When I began my search for a rescue dog I had certain criteria, deal breakers if you will. Based on 47 years of Labrador parenting these seemed like reasonable requirements to me. Thus, the list.

1. No dogs from my sister's sanctuary in Kansas

2. No dogs from photograph

3. No terrier mixes

4. No small dogs

5. No dogs with aggression toward other animals or humans

6. No health issues

But then I started to rethink my rules. My sister runs a sanctuary for abandoned and abused dogs and no one is more dedicated or fearless in her rescues. When there is no more room at the inn she relies on foster homes as a temporary measure. I check her web page often (in the spirit of window shopping only) and my eye fell on a little black dog dressed in a toddler's t-shirt, pink underpants and a tutu. OK, "small" could be good—a dog I could carry, lift into the car, help

over snow drifts, walk in a civilized fashion. So I took her picture to work where the reaction was unanimous. "Have you lost your mind?" "Does she need those underpants?" "You're joking, right?"

Fast forward. I am in the air freight terminal in Washington, D.C., two hours early, eagerly awaiting the plane from Kansas and, finally, out of a new $85 crate (air fare C.O.D.) steps a very confident, non-frequent flyer; short, but by no means small. Clearly I am losing control of this list. From the beginning, my house became her command post, and she rules with an iron fist. Dinner at 6:30 sharp—boneless chicken, green beans and cottage cheese. If I am late, by 6:40 she is stomping her feet, by 6:50 she has kicked her food bowl across the floor. She strides through the house like a Samurai Warrior with shoulders like an NFL linebacker. Bedtime at 10:30, accompanied by two treats, a footstool and an electric fan. Reveille at 7:00 a.m., including weekends. She hates other dogs and small children. She is probably the cutest dog I have ever seen.

Pippa, newly named, had a murky background; pieced together, it told the story of a survivor. This was, and is, a tough little dog who was first spotted being thrown from a car in a snowstorm with her chum, a little black and white Boston Terrier (?). A woman driving by scooped up the freezing dogs, turned her heater up and drove to the nearest shelter, unfortunately one with a high kill rate. The Boston Terrier mix had some interested adopters; the other identified only as "Jo," written on a piece of paper tied to a tattered string around her neck, was not going to be so lucky. And then someone thought to call SCARS. Since they were full, my sister found a foster home for Jo. So, I was about to get a new dog who didn't meet a single requirement on my list. Oh, I forgot to tell you. Pippa has diabetes and gets two insulin shots a day.

We have lived in harmony for 11 years. I sometimes worry that her antisocial behavior limits her fun— no dog parks, Halloween parties, visits with Santa, play dates—but she seems perfectly content in the universe she has created for herself. She surveys the street from her perch on the back of the couch (white) and patrols the large back yard on foot. Once a day she begrudgingly accompanies her dog walker (expensive) around the block if the coast is clear. She watches television on a blanket at my feet and sleeps in my bed with her head on the pillow and one arm clutching mine. She defends me against all enemies foreign and domestic, and vacuum cleaners.

I love my little Tooter Tot. What good is an old list anyway!

PENNY

trudy

This is a sad story. I wrote it 30 years ago and it still makes me cry. But I was young and inexperienced in the heartbreak of animal rescue, and I have learned much since then. Many of the dogs that have passed through our doors did not live out their allotted years—their bodies were too broken to save—but every one of them died with loving arms around them and that was my reward. The world is full of cruel people, but countless good Samaritans hit their brakes every day on a highway or country road and save a dog who was thrown out , tied in a hefty bag or just frightened and lost , or feed and water a neighbor's dog who is neglected, and reach out in a multitude of ways to alleviate suffering. This gives me hope that one day our sad stories will all have happy endings.

TRUDY

It was a warm November day when Trudy died. Most of the leaves had fallen from the trees, and people were raking them into piles in their yards. It didn't seem fair that she, who had been deprived of sunlight for so long, should leave us on such a day.

Trudy came into our lives when we received a call from a Marla Rodgers who lived in central Kansas and was desperate for help. Forty six dogs on a few acres, and Marla was being evicted. What was the deal here? As we pieced the story together, a picture began forming in our minds, and it wasn't good. Eccentric woman, starving dogs, animal hoarder, eviction notices. I didn't like it. Although she was in a neighboring county, it was still within the jurisdiction of our humane society. This would involve hours of driving, and we were a small shelter, dreadfully short of money and help.

But she kept calling, and calling. She was getting more desperate. Marla begged us to rescue her dogs, she had no one else to turn to. One afternoon Ed, our volunteer and local fireman, stopped by the office at the shelter. He had done some abuse investigation for us in the past, and we told him this story. He replied, "I've been there, and it is bad. Don't you remember when I got the call from the sheriff in a neighboring county? The dogs live in filth and most are padlocked to steel drums outside. Those are the lucky ones. The rest live in old sheds in the dark, and have been there for years and recoil at the sight of humans. You two women couldn't handle it, you would get sick and leave."

With that, I looked at my co- director, Colleen. I could tell by her face that he had kindled something in us, and it was taking hold. After all, weren't we both Irish? Colleen and Maureen? I knew in that moment that no matter how much we protested, we would go to Marla's and would not leave until every last dog was saved.

Borrowing three vans and rounding up ten volunteers, we were ready to move the dogs to safety. Blankets, buckets of water, food and crates were loaded in the vehicles, and we prepared the staff for the arrival of 46 new dogs, some of whom would need immediate medical care. Makeshift kennels were set up, resident dogs reorganized, and all was in place. We were ready to roll.

Days later when our mission was accomplished, we settled into a routine back at the shelter and discussed our newest residents.

"Colleen, do you remember the first time we saw Trudy chained outside of that dark shed?" I asked. Colleen smiled and nodded. Trudy would live forever in the memory of those who had been there. Her white, wavy coat had stood out in the back of that dark room. Had it not been for her coat, amazingly still lustrous, we might have missed her in the rubble.

There were six or eight dogs chained and padlocked in that particular section, and we wondered how long they had waited in that dim light, waited for a hand to release them from their bondage. We would find out that most had waited for a long time. They had that confused, squinting look in their eyes that told, more than words could, how long they had been held prisoner.

Blonde and spritely, Trudy was a small collie mix of about ten pounds with a thick feathered tail that curled up like a plume. She was a perfect lady, shy and reticent, never pushy. When I came into the shelter in the mornings, the dogs would jump and bark in unison, but not Trudy. Sitting back, eyes holding mine, she would tentatively wag her tail. Like so many of these dogs, she was reserved and self disciplined. Years of neglect, poor diet, and little companionship had taken its toll.

One Sunday afternoon when the work was done and the animals were resting, I took a treasured moment to sit on the floor and hold Trudy. She gently rested her head against my shoulder, put her paw on my arm and closed her eyes. A few moments later, a couple from Wichita looked in and asked if we were still open. They were looking for a small house dog, and the husband kept looking at Trudy. I pulled myself up and showed them some of our small dogs.

"We recently received a large number of dogs from a nearby county and many are small. They are not all housebroken yet, but it shouldn't take too long. The beige one is Heather, and she is a loving Pekingnese mix. She has come a long way from hiding and shaking and now runs up to strangers and wags her tail. The black and tan one is Penny, and she is lively, smart, healthy and her teeth are not decayed like some of the others. Perhaps she was not there for too long. This one is Trudy, and she is our favorite here at the shelter," and I scooped her up in my arms. Mr. Allen looked at his wife and said, "She is beautiful, and you can tell how gentle she is." However, his wife and son seemed to be leaning toward Penny.

I explained that we had noticed some questionable areas on Trudy's tummy anyway, and I wanted to take her to the vet before we adopted her out. That seemed to make their decision easier, and they adopted Penny. The Allens filled out the adoption form, paid the fee, and I tied a pink ribbon on Penny's neck. She was all set, and I gave her a squeeze and sent up a silent prayer that she would work out for them.

The next morning when I got a break, I drove over to the vet to get Trudy checked out. I should have been more worried than I was, for he was certain the lumps were malignant. The biopsy would be painful, the surgery worse, and hadn't she suffered enough already? And there was always the specter that looms over every humane society......not enough money.

Driving back to the shelter with Trudy, I kept hoping Colleen would be there. Her good judgement and sensible attitude, combined with her deep love for animals, would make her the best person to help me make a decision. We agreed on the inevitable. She stoically took her to the clinic and I stayed back, lacking the courage to go.

Two hours later, Colleen and I had to go back to the clinic for some supplies. I hoped it would be over for Trudy, but it wasn't. The vet had been incredibly busy and Trudy was still in the cage, frightened and alone. We asked if she could be given a tranquilizer shot which he often gave us, free of charge, out of his compassion for the shelter animals. We had a neglected calf to check out, so we took Trudy with us while her shot took effect.

I could hardly drive for looking at her precious face. She lay on her back in Colleen's arms, resting quietly with her eyes drooping. Her tiny feet were near me, and as I held and stroked one of them, I noticed for the first time how fragile and light they were. She drowsed in the sun that shone through the car window with the beautiful Kansas countryside rolling by. What a well kept secret this land was with its rich wheat fields and winding country roads. This was Trudy's birthright, but one she could not claim. She had never had the simple joy a dog should have of chasing a rabbit or romping in a field. Oh, what a good feeling it would have been to say at least her five short years were good ones, but this was not to be. Her life had been spent surviving hard, unrelenting Kansas winters with inadequate shelter, and the beautiful summer days were denied her within that broken down, dark shed. If there was any consolation in this, it was that we spared her dying slowly and painfully in that cruel environment.

When it was all over, we put her gently in a box in a curled sleeping position and covered her with a light blue towel. Colleen took Trudy home to the country where the air was fresh and clean and her horses grazed peacefully in the pasture. She buried her next to a shelter dog who had been killed in an accident, hoping they would be good friends.

Spring has finally come to Kansas again. It has been a long, hard winter with sub zero temperatures, late snows, and cold winds blowing across the plains. I don't think of Trudy every single day now, and it has been awhile since I have cried about her. But on a sunny day, when I am driving in the country, I like to imagine that I see her romping through a field of sunflowers with her plumed tail waving behind her.

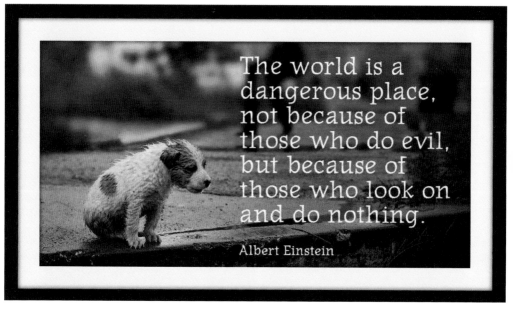

The world is a dangerous place, not because of those who do evil, but because of those who look on and do nothing.

Albert Einstein